Other Works by Bethany Davis:

The Moon and Stars of the Dark Night Sky (Book I)

THE CHASM OF MIST

POEMS OF THE LONGING OF CELESTE FOR HER SOPHIA

THE MOON AND STARS OF THE DARK NIGHT SKY

BOOK II

BETHANY DAVIS

Caer Illandria Enterprises
P.O. Box 7557, Broomfield, CO 80021
www.caerillandria.com

Copyright © 2017 by Bethany Davis

All poems copyright © 2015 by Bethany Davis

All rights reserved.

Printed in the United States of America

First Edition

Ingram Printing

ISBN: 0998620009
ISBN-13: 978-0998620008

For my Sophia, my Dark Night Sky, my Muse, my Song. It's been a long hard journey, and the time during which I wrote these poems was dark, not in the way of the Night, but of mists of uncertainty. The chasm that separated us, it was harder than anything I have ever had to endure, and our reunion when at last I was in your arms again, it made all the mist worthwhile. This book, these poems, they are our separation and our return, both through the ages and during that hard season. My muse, my Sophia, thank you for waiting, for always coming back.

CONTENTS

SAFE AT HOME SECURE	1
LIMINAL I STAND	3
HEARTBEATS	5
SWOONING	7
SPRINGTIME'S PROMISED RAIN	9
HOMEWARD BOUND	11
UPON THE STORMY SEA	13
LIKE A BUTTERFLY	15
READING POETRY TO THE DEAD	17
MATED GEESE	19
FLYING SOUTH FOR SPRING	21
HEART'S DELIGHT	23
BLOOD ON FIRE	25
BUILDING DOORS	27
DAPPLED MORNING LIGHT	29
WHIMSICAL	31
SUNLIT SKIES	33
THE FLUX	35
CELESTE'S MOODS	37
ENDLESS SEARCHES AND	39
WHAT IS FOUND	39
THE THOUGHTS AND DREAMS	41
AS ONE	43
WANDERING	45
EACH NIGHT	47
I WAIT FOR DUSK	49
THE DARK NIGHT SKY	51
RABBIT HOLES	53
YOUR KISS IS BLISS	55
ALL AROUND	57
BLOOD RED ROSE	59
NYCTOPHILIA	61
THE PLACE I LONG	63
PLASTIC ROSES	65
DEPTHS OF YOU	67
MIST AND SMOKE	69

Absence is to love what wind is to fire; it
extinguishes the small, it inflames the great.
— Roger de Rabutin de Bussy

The Chasm of Mist

Safe at Home Secure

In your arms, I long to be, each breath a breath that's shared,
Skin on skin in cool night air, each move a sweet caress,
Drifting in and out of sleep, but knowing you're right there,
Safe we are with our own true loves, safe at home secure.

Hold me, love, as I lie awake, hold me as I sleep,
Breath my breathe and let me breathe, the air that is your breath,
Touch me love and feel my skin, caress my soft warm skin,
Safe we are with our own true loves, safe at home secure.

When I move and walk and pace, it's never very far,
And soon I return to your sweet arms, that hold me in the dark,
Nowhere else I long to be, but only with my love,
Safe we are with our own true loves, safe at home secure.

~April 13, 2015

Bethany Davis

Liminal I Stand

Liminal I stand,
Standing here in limbo,
The chasm stretches oh so very wide.

It stretches wide,
The gap she widens,
Standing here in grey no-man's land.

Neither here nor there,
Neither there nor here.
And the mist it rises higher and higher still.

She rises up,
Up she rises,
A misty serpent with a burning head of fire.

Burning in me,
Burning in her,
Burning in that cold grey chasm full of mist.

Rising higher,
Steam from below,
Blocking my only view of my one true love.

How can I cross it,
Where is the bridge,
To finally reach my heart, my own true love?

~April 30, 2015

Bethany Davis

Heartbeats

I long for her heartbeat,
Like a pounding drum,
Like pouring rain in the night,
I listen, I wait,
Wait to find her bed again,
Our bed again,
As I leave the mountains,
Leave this place of crowds and cars,
Leave the hustle and bustle of a city,
Laid out below the shadow of the Flatirons,
Stretching to the plains,
Leave and drive,
Drive to the prairies of the north,
Drive to her arms,
Drive to that heartbeat,
Like lightning across the sky,
Across my mind,
Across my soul,
Where I lay in her arms and listen,
Listen to her heart in the night,
Her leather, my lace,
One, lost, forgotten on the floor,
As my finger traces each curve,
Each bone,
Each muscle,
Traces like a paintbrush,
Light as a feather,
On the canvas of her skin,
Light across the tattoos,
That glow with meaning,
Her painted canvas,
Not just skin but soul,
Her strong arms holding my body,
Warming my cold body,
Warming my blood,
Until it burns like Irish whiskey,
Down my throat on a cold rainy day,
And I sigh,

Bethany Davis

In my mind at her touch,
In my memory at her touch,
In my anticipation and desire,
And I sigh in my old room alone,
And I pack,
I prepare,
To leave the mountains I've called home,
Leave the fair Flatirons,
Leave the towering Frontrange,
Leave the plains,
Leave the view of the white peaks,
Of the Colorado Rockies,
Leave this place that was home,
But is no longer,
Leave and drive,
Drive to the rolling prairies,
The dancing, living skies,
Drive to the northern prairies,
Fair and beautiful Saskatchewan,
Drive to her,
Who always holds my attention,
Whom I hold's attention,
Just by living and breathing,
Two heartbeats as one,
Beneath hot skin on a cold night,
I leave this place,
And go,
Home.

~ April 19, 2015

Swooning

A purr,
A word,
A sound,
Vibrating through me,
Like a tuning fork,
Perfect pitch,
Not of a song,
Not of a melody,
Not of harmony,
The resonance of my soul,
My heart,
My all,
I swoon,
Like a fair lady,
At the knight's brave words,
The poet's whisper,
Her true love's kiss,
Swooning,
Soul ablaze,
Heart ablaze,
Logic and proportion,
Fallen,
Lost,
Lost in her voice,
Lost in her,
Fighting to breathe,
Fighting for words,
Flushed and swooning,
Her maiden,
Her kitten,
Lost in her voice,
The sound,
Like a bow across fiddle strings,
The first note purring,
The cry,
Of tears and joy,
Laughter and sorry,
Slow and steady,

Bethany Davis

Ringing out across the expanse,
Of the chasm,
Open and gaping,
Echoing,
My heart strings,
My hot centre,
Hot for her,
A purring tomcat,
Unaware of her voice,
Drawn softly but firmly across my strings,
Like the touch I long for,
Desire,
Want,
Need,
Like a note,
Perfect and pure,
That tuning fork,
That draws out the marching note in my soul,
Mournful and joyful,
All of me,
Ringing for all of her,
Vibrating,
A sound,
A word,
A purr.

~April 19, 2015

Springtime's Promised Rain

I say goodbye to the Flatirons fair,
I sail across the plains,
To the northern prairies of golden grain,
And to my love's arms.

Spring has come, and with it change,
And for me more than most,
And like the blossoming prairie flowers,
I blossom as I go.

Green buds of spring and bright bright flowers,
And the late frosts now and then,
Spring's fair promise that calls to me,
As I head finally home.

And her I seek who makes me blush,
Whom wakes my giggles fair,
To her I go and leave behind,
All that has come before.

Like blowing hair in blowing wind,
I rush and flow to her,
And chilly springtime's promised rain,
And promises of sun.

And spring it is the time to go,
The time to reach my home,
The welcoming arms of my lover's joy,
Upon prairie waves of grain.

So I say goodbye to Flatirons fair,
I sail across the plains,
To the northern prairies of golden grain,
And to my love's arms.

Spring has come, and with it change,
And for me more than most,
And like the blossoming prairie flowers,

Bethany Davis

I blossom as I go.

~April 20, 2015

The Chasm of Mist

Homeward Bound

I'm far away but I draw near,
In time if not in space,
It gets so hard with each new day,
When I'm neither there nor here,
Homeward bound with each new breath,
Soon I'll see your face,
Though every moment is hard as fuck,
I'll soon be homeward bound.

The mountain light and mountain call,
It fades with each passing day,
And the prairie wind it calls my name,
Calling me to come on home,
To you my love and to your arms,
I'm seeking to come home,
Though every moment is hard as hell,
I'll soon be homeward bound.

In the dark a lantern raised,
For me to see afar,
My own true love she calls to me,
Calls me to come on home,
And in the night when I'm all alone,
And in the blinding sun,
Though every moment is hard as fuck,
I'll soon be homeward bound.

You are my one, my only one,
You are my own truly love,
You ground me, hold me, light my fire,
You call my rushing wind,
Like water from the mountains high,
I rush toward the plains,
Though every moment is hard as hell,
I'll soon be homeward bound.

~April 21, 2015

Bethany Davis

The Chasm of Mist

Upon the Stormy Sea

I sail across a stormy sea,
Between two distant shores,
A sea of mist and smoke and dreams,
Is all beneath my hull,
I'm neither there or neither here,
But somewhere in between,
And though I sail before the gales,
My progress it is slow.

I sail across a stormy sea,
Of smoke and mists and dreams,
No bottom there nor naught below,
No fish or reefs or sand,
Out here where I'm all alone,
Bending to the wheel,
But soon I'll come to that far shore,
Where is my only love.

I sail across a stormy sea,
With no bottom I can see,
The shore behind is growing dim,
But I'm still lost at sea,
A chasm deep of mist and smoke,
My boat is pushing hard,
To reach the shore of my true love,
In the distance now I see.

I sail across a stormy sea,
Away from the shore I left,
And though I push as hard as hell
It's slow I come to her,
And in morning light I see that shore,
And know I'll reach that far far port,
Until then I push before the gale,
Upon this stormy sea.

~April 22, 2015

Bethany Davis

Like a Butterfly

The love in me for you dances,
Fluttering in the wind like a butterfly,
Rising up from deep within,
From a gentle breeze to a roaring gale,
It rises, rises, and spreads it's delicate wings,
Delicate but strong, mighty, might like the gale,
And the flutter, excited, free, crazy as a loon in the gale,
Flutter for new adventures and memories shared,
Flutter for the unknown and what is known too well,
Flutter for the love of you that fills me,
Like my beating heart, rushing each time we kiss,
Rushing, rising, rushing like that mighty gale,
And my wings spread and I fly, fly with you,
On wings that flutter like a butterfly.

~April 22, 2015

Bethany Davis

The Chasm of Mist

Reading Poetry to the Dead

There's beauty there in Death's dark eyes,
Calling strong and true,
Never fading ever raging,
Toward Death's black Gate,
I see her wings of shadow spread,
Wings both dark and true,
And desperation in that dark place,
Devouring all my world,
What do I do, what can I do,
To keep my lover dark?
I'll be with her, it's all I can,
With her there out of reach,
Let it be us, not her alone,
As time starts to stand still,
Black wolf raging, for all is lost,
The darkness in her eyes,
All I want is to hold and have her,
There beneath her wings,
Poetry it comes and finds me,
And is my one escape,
If it's the end let it be like that,
My words in her ears,
And to I read, both light and rending,
The words that are of us,
It's all I have, my one last gift,
Before she parts the Veil,
And in her eyes that darkness glowing,
A beauty none have seen,
My love, my heart, my soul and lover,
With wings of shadow spread,
Poetry echoes in word and mind,
Of all our wandering nights,
And if I lose her let it be me present,
And not her all alone,
For all the years and all the lifetimes,
Are all in just one breath,
And her and I, the night and moonlight,

Bethany Davis

And all the blazing stars,
And in the shadow of the Gates of Death,
She's slipping from my grasp,
And in that place where Life's dark shadow,
Is brighter than the sun,
The edges quiver and shake in darkness,
The Veil is very thin,
And the Gates of Death there open widely,
Call and call again,
But in her eyes, the darkness changes,
For she can't care for me,
And there we linger and she steps backwards,
And the Gates are shut again,
But I'll remember for all my breaths and moments,
And many days to come,
The beauty death had painted on her,
The shadow of herself,
The life is beauty and death is too,
And all that comes between,
In the secret chamber before the gates,
Where I read poetry to the Dead.

~April 30, 2015

Mated Geese

Like mated geese,
In flight above,
Migrating to the north,
I came to you,
In hope and faith,
Sure of my sacred flight.

My one true love,
My mated goose,
The one I'll ever love,
I came to you,
In hope and faith,
Sure of my sacred flight.

Through stormy skies,
I flew to you,
And all I had to give,
I came to you,
In hope and faith,
Sure of my sacred flight.

But there I was,
Stuck in mid flight,
Stopped so close to you,
I came to you,
In hope and faith,
Sure of my sacred flight.

My wings are clipped,
My flight is stopped
And I so far from you,
I came to you,
In hope and faith,
Sure of my sacred flight.

But time will pass,
And I will come,
My wings then fully healed,

Bethany Davis

I came to you,
In hope and faith,
Sure of my sacred flight.

And then I'll be,
There by your side,
Each and every night,
I'll come to you,
My hope, my faith,
Sure of my sacred flight.

~May 11, 2015

The Chasm of Mist

Flying South for Spring

South I fled like winter storms,
The thunder crashing round,
Sorrow and pain they were my fare,
Like coins upon my eyes.
Two gold coins to pay my way,
On Charon's wooden boat.

Just like the Dead on the River Styx,
And mist of lives long past,
Across that water I did sail,
The rain was falling fast,
From my love I was forced to flee,
A fate much worse than death.

To the south I did return,
Once home was now exile,
And all the beauty and lovely things,
Had faded into grey,
For I was then so far from home,
Back to my former home.

North it is geese are meant to fly,
In the early days of spring,
But South I went away from her,
Who makes my own soul sing,
Death's wide door was open far,
When to the South I went.

Why do the pains of living things,
Help us to know we live,
And why does that river of the Dead,
Speak of living things,
And gold coins paid my sorrowful way,
On Charon's wooden boat.

~May 20, 2015

Bethany Davis

Heart's Delight

You are my love,
My heart's delight,
You make my blood run hot.

I long for you,
Both day and night,
I long for your sweet embrace.

The time has been,
The time will come,
When I sleep there in your arms.

And for that day,
I yearn and pray,
And can't wait until it comes.

~April 27, 2015

Bethany Davis

Blood on Fire

Sunlight plays with burning fingers,
And dances all divine,
And brings to mind my lover's touch,
And how I burn for her,
I want you love, your loving touch,
I want your holding arms,
I want to kiss your burning lips,
And set your blood on fire,
My longing burns and will come true,
For I can't now let it not,
And all my soul and all my blood,
It burns for your embrace,
Through mazes long and forests dark,
And desolate empty plains,
I seek the way, the path that leads there,
To your strong holding arms,
And I will find it and come back home,
My exile finally done,
And kiss those lips that burn with passion,
And eyes that light my own.

~April 30, 2015

Bethany Davis

Building Doors

One by one, I build the doors,
That will lead me there to you,
Each door built is one more way,
To pass that chasm deep,
I build a door then build some more,
And only one I'll need,
But each door built might be the one,
That leads me there to you.

One by one, I build the doors,
That will lead me there to you,
A thousand keys and for each a lock,
And one lock in every door,
I'll try the keys and see which one,
Will open the way for me,
But each key tried might be the one,
That leads me there to you.

One by one, I build the doors,
That will lead me there to you,
The process long and work is hard,
The long waiting for that day,
But each door built and each key tried,
Is worth that final goal,
And each long sigh might be the one,
That leads me there to you.

One by one, I build the doors,
That will lead me there to you,
The misty chasm may open wide,
But I will build a bridge,
To cross the depths to your loving arms,
And open that way for me,
But each bridge built might be the one,
That leads me there to you.

~May 11, 2015

Bethany Davis

Dappled Morning Light

Morning dappled light on pale, pale skin,
Lit by my glow, not the light of day,
My glowing love, glowing bright for you,
Lighting you in the dappled morning light.

Sweet love that shines in dappled shining light,
And glows within with each beat of my heart,
My love it grows with each new light of day,
Lighting you in the dappled morning light.

So sweet your kiss in the dappled light of day,
And in the deep dark shadows of the night,
I come to you in waking and in dream,
Lighting you in the dappled morning light.

My lover sweet, you make me glow so bright,
By your touch and kiss in the morning dappled light,
I miss you so when we are far apart,
And I long for you in the dappled morning light.

And memory and hope and thoughts and dreams,
Are so real and vivid in the morning light,
My longing is so strong in the middle of the night,
And I long for you in the dappled morning light.

And when I view you from close or from afar,
And dappled light plays playfully across your face,
My kiss should be firmly planted there,
And light you in the dappled morning light.

~May 16, 2015

Bethany Davis

Whimsical

Whimsical and silly,
Wistful and floating,
I sigh,
I settle,
I dance in the sky,
And laze lightly,
Calm,
Relaxed,
No worries at all,
As I read to my love,
The poetry from my heart.

~May 16, 2015

Bethany Davis

Sunlit Skies

Sunlit skies of blue and white,
And bright green leaves of spring,
A peaceful morning in bright sunlight,
A morning here with you.

No sky or clouds or trees or views,
Ever could compare with you,
The peace I find in your loving arms,
The peace when I bring a smile to you.

I miss you love like I'd miss the world,
If I was past the Gates,
I miss your touch and your loving kiss,
And the quiet peace we shared.

Soon I will come back to my home,
And your warm loving arms,
And the peace I find in sky and cloud,
Will fade compared to you.

My love is like the blowing wind,
That nothing can slow down,
My love is like the clouds so high,
That are most never bound.

My love for you is like the trees,
That reach up for the sky,
My love for you is like the leaves,
Bright vibrant and alive.

Like the breeze now through my growing hair,
That makes me wistful and alit,
My love for you is like that breeze,
And filled with great delight.

A nice spring morning on a lovely day,
With you there for me to see,
Is a delight both now and then,

Bethany Davis

Is better than when we're apart.

But love, my heart, and my delight,
The dark love of my life,
In your arms I long to be,
Both now and every night.

I'll come to you like the morning breeze,
I'll come like the free and moving clouds,
I'll seek your arms and your loving kiss,
Like the trees reach for the shining sun.

Sunlit skies of blue and white,
And bright green leaves of spring,
A peaceful morning in bright sunlight,
A morning here with you.

No sky or clouds or trees or views,
Ever could compare with you,
The peace I find in your loving arms,
The peace when I bring a smile to you.

~May 17, 2015

The Flux

The flux that flows in living things,
In liminal space and time,
It moves and grows and shrinks again,
Through cracks in all our lives,
And as it flows it seems to me,
That nothing stays the same,
Moving cracks and floating shards,
Throughout all eternity,
But what oh wait what, the flux,
We know it's true,
Change does come, it cracks and creeks,
Through souls oh stars souls and through our hearts,
Like water
  and like quick, quick sand,
    like dust in a blowing wind,
     Fire burns,
       Lightning strikes,
      And flux it causes change,
   In and out,
Between broad cracks,
 Flowing,
  Moving,
Flux,
Shards and cracks,
 cupboard doors,
stars and moon and night,
 dark, dark light,
light, light, dark,
 The Chasm open wide,
What,
 Oh wait,
  What will come next,
   When cracks are open wide,
And in our souls,
 Oh stars they are,
  In souls and in the cracks,
All the flux and changing things,
Will come all rushing back,

Bethany Davis

And from the change and from the flux,
Things will be calm again,
And in the new found settled world,
I'll rest in my lover's arms,
And though the flux is all around,
In all us living things,
I'll be with you real soon my love,
I'll know your precious kiss,
For what might change and all the flux,
Though hard to handle now,
Is only the most truest path,
Till we are forever near.

~May 23, 2015

Celeste's Moods

Longing comes,
It ebbs and flows,
Like the waning and the waxing moon,

Like Celeste's moods
In dark night sky,
That come and go again,

I long for you,
For your touch,
At midnight and at noon,

And for you kiss,
I pine and long,
In mountains and the plains,

And when I come,
And hold you tight,
I will love you for all eternity.

~May 25, 2015

Bethany Davis

Endless Searches and What is Found

Through windless plains or roaring gales,
There's no place I wouldn't go,
Mountains high and seas so low,
And forests dense as night.

The endless plains of infinite grass,
That stretch beyond the Veil,
I'd search them on for all of time,
Until my search was done.

And endless forests so dense and dark,
With all manner of dangers and fears,
I'd search beneath each living root,
And to each tall tree top.

The endless sea with out an end,
With no stars to guide my course,
I'd sail for years or lifetimes more,
from sea to shining sea.

The endless mountains so tall and proud,
That clouds do hide the tops,
I'd climb each cliff despite the heights,
And search round each living rock.

Until I found what I have found,
For which I need not search,
My loving love, my lover dark,
You whom I most adore.

~June 2, 2015

Bethany Davis

The Thoughts and Dreams

I think of you both night and day,
  As I travel on and on,
The journey stretches and wears on me,
  But of you I always dream,
I long for you in mornings fair,
  And in the driving rain,
And some day soon,
  The thoughts and dreams,
Will be reality.

You hold my thoughts both night and day,
  If I'm moving or staying still,
If my days are full with busy things,
  Or if I've naught to do,
I long for you when I'm working hard,
  And when I'm all alone,
And some day soon,
  The thoughts and dreams,
Will be reality.

Each word you speak and every quirk,
  Of eye or mouth or chin,
They stick with me like treasures fair,
  And consume my thoughts,
Each thing you do and say and think,
  Is all I want and need,
And some day soon,
  The thoughts and dreams,
Will be reality.

You are my love and all my dreams,
  The darkened sky at night,
And the mist-filled chasm stretches wide,
  Soon I'll hold you tight,
My arms now long but soon will hold,
  My love so very tight,
And some day soon,
  The thoughts and dreams,

Will be reality.

~June 9, 2015

As One

In your arms I long to be,
Both now and for eternity,
It matters not where we lay our heads,
Or where we watch the rising sun,
As long as we lay as one.

If it's a wheeled house far away,
And we are out there raising sheep,
I'll smile and watch your gentle hand,
As you love and care for them,
As long as we lay as one.

If it's a sailboat out on the sea,
Or sitting on some lonely dock,
You'll smile and watch wind in my hair,
As I gaze out at all there is,
As long as we lay as one.

If it's a farmhouse on a peaceful lane,
With plants and animals all around,
I'll smile and watch you wipe your brow,
As we work the dark rich ground,
As long as we lay as one.

If it's a high-rise in the land of steel,
Or a suburban house like all around,
You'll take my hand and we'll walk awhile,
Content that we aren't alone,
As long as we lay as one.

For in your arms I long to be,
Both now and for eternity,
It matters not where we lay our heads,
Or where we watch the rising sun,
As long as we lay as one.

~June 10, 2015

Bethany Davis

Wandering

Of you I think as my mind does roam,
  And wanders all the hills,
    Of your soft touch and strong embrace,
     Of all the worlds within,

My lover sweet and darkness deep,
  And the one who longs for me,
    How sweet your lips and your caress,
     In the darkness of the night,

Though many places I tend to roam,
  So desolate and so dark,
    Within my mind when I wander lost,
     But it's you I know I'll find,

Those barren hills and mountain peaks,
  And forests dark as pitch,
    Across that sea and the chasm of mist,
     And everywhere between,

It's to your arms I will always go,
  And there I long to be,
    And when you hold me once again,
     Your missing will call your name.

~June 24, 2015

Bethany Davis

Each Night

Each night I long and pine for you,
Each morning I marvel on,
Each day I think and wish for you,
Each evening my want is you.

In darkest night I know you're there,
In shadows deep and worried sleep,
In each moment of the deepest night,
In love with you my lover dark.

To morning light I always return,
To sunlight shining bright,
To each fair moment to know your love,
To all that is all us.

All day I think of nothing else,
All moments I wish for you,
All things to show and things to share,
All the time we have.

As shadows fall each evening come,
As we return to night,
As I wish for only you,
As much as all there is.

Each night I long and pine for you,
Each morning I marvel on,
Each day I think and wish for you,
Each evening my want is you.

~June 25, 2015

Bethany Davis

I Wait for Dusk

Each one who makes my baby wait,
Should go and fuck themselves,
For each moment she waits around,
Is one more we spend apart.

Why does this life always make us wait,
And waste that precious time,
That we could be holding each other tight,
And feel each other's touch?

I wait and wait and you do too,
For the day when waiting's done,
And each long moment stretches long,
Like shadows in the dusk.

It will be soon, my heart, my soul,
When all the waiting's done,
I'll hold you close, you'll hold me tight,
And I'll kiss you in the dusk.

~July 6, 2015

Bethany Davis

The Dark Night Sky

The dark night sky,
Where I long to be,
Where my stars shine,
And my moon is full,
Of her I think,
In noon day sun,
Of her I think,
In the darkest nights,
The sky may rain,
And the sky may storm,
Snow might fall,
Or great big hail,
But in her arms,
I always shine,
The moon and stars,
Of the dark night sky.

~July 8, 2015

Bethany Davis

Rabbit Holes

In Wonderland I'm apt to walk,
And wander through the hills,
My wanderlust within myself,
For places never seen,
Deep I go down rabbit holes,
And follow where they lead,
And where they go no one knows,
Or where the rabbit leads.

In Wanderland I'm apt to walk,
And wonder about the world,
Of why my love is far away,
Or why the world's so hard,
Each step we take is like that fall,
Down that long rabbit hole,
Down and down it seems to go,
But closer we become.

In Wanderlust I'm apt to walk,
My mind never quite stays still,
It wanders on and wonders on,
And goes so far away,
But I will walk through flower beds,
Or through giant key hole doors,
And stand before the Queen of Hearts,
If you are by my side.

In Wonderlust I'm apt to walk,
For I know nothing else,
This Alice fair, this bright Celeste,
Will find you waiting there,
Hand in hand we face the world,
Though sometimes we are lost,
But with each step and down each hole,
I know you're always here.

In Wonderland I'm apt to walk,
And wander through the hills,

Bethany Davis

My wanderlust within myself,
For places never seen,
Deep I go down rabbit holes,
And follow where they lead,
And where they go no one knows,
Or where the rabbit leads.

~July 10, 2015

Your Kiss is Bliss

Your kiss was bliss and will be again,
When you kiss my lips once more,
Your arms around me holding tight,
Before and soon once more,
It's you I love and long and pine,
For each look or touch or kiss,
And nothing else I want or need,
Just you and me with you.

My kiss was bliss when I tasted yours,
And I long for another drink,
When at last we're side by side,
Or pressed against the other,
For that day I wait and long,
Sometimes patient sometimes not,
For nothing else I want or need,
Just you and you with me.

Our kiss was bliss when it we shared,
And soon we'll taste again,
Each day we wait is one more near,
Each night one closer still,
For soon my love my heart and soul,
We'll hold each other close,
For nothing else I want or need,
Just us and you with me.

~July 10, 2015

Bethany Davis

All Around

All around I'm apt to go,
And think of all the ways,
But only to my own true love,
Do my thought return again,
She is all that I desire and want,
And the one I truly need,
And each day my own strange heart,
Grows more in love with her,
She's like the monkshood in the shade,
In shadows, almost black,
Few see the beauty or the power,
Of the flower they avoid,
She's like the darkness beneath the trees,
In the densest forest lands,
The light comes not but the night can see,
The beauty beneath the bows,
She I see and her alone,
Forevermore I shall,
I don't give a fuck what others see,
Or if they try at all,
I love my love in shadowed lands,
And in the bright day sun,
I love her true in all her moods,
And in all of mine,
Strange am I and so is she,
And others can never know,
The joy I find in her embrace,
Or in her haunting gaze,
All around I'm apt to go,
And think of all the ways,
But only to my own true love,
Do my thought return again,
She is all that I desire and want,
And the one I truly need,
And each day my own strange heart,
Grows more in love with her.

~July 19, 2015

Bethany Davis

Blood Red Rose

I've heard is said and oft compared,
Love to a bright red rose,
And I've tasted of and know the sting,
Of the thorny blood red rose,
Your thorns my dear are part of you,
And I love them just as much,
As the blood red beauty of your loveliness,
That red that's touching black,
Thorns I know and have transgressed,
The thicket and the hedge,
And your thorns I love much more,
And the beauty of your rose,
For rose you are in darkened light,
The red of dark dark blood,
I see the beauty you try to hide,
And see most all of you,
A rose is sweet they're oft to say,
But don't know of the sting,
For each rose that they dare to smell,
Has had them long removed,
And all the roses that they smell,
That they say are so sweet,
Are tame and bland and barely smell,
Are safe and held at bay,
But you my love are a wild rose,
And strong and free and wild,
Your thorns may prick me to the core,
But your petals I love the more,
And there is nothing about you love,
That's tame or bland or safe,
And I love you for your thorns my dear,
And for your dark beauty,
And blood may run from sharp thorn tip,
And match the blood red rose,
And all who know who truly know,
Will never ever forget,
For the blood rose grows in wild space,
And shadowed unsafe lands,

Bethany Davis

And with each day grows wild and free,
And ever more my love,
I've heard is said and oft compared,
Love to a bright red rose,
And I've tasted of and know the sting,
Of the thorny blood red rose,
Your thorns my dear are part of you,
And I love them just as much,
As the blood red beauty of your loveliness,
That red that's touching black.

~July 19, 2015

Nyctophilia

My love of darkness,
My love of you,
My amazing dark night sky.

Lost I get,
And found in you,
My amazing dark night sky.

For you I long,
For you I pine,
My amazing dark night sky.

The day is long,
When I'm at work,
My amazing dark night sky.

But when it's done,
I see your face,
My amazing dark night sky.

The stars they come,
The stars they go,
My amazing dark night sky.

The moon it wanes,
And waxes out,
My amazing dark night sky.

But there you are,
For me to find,
My amazing dark night sky.

And in the night,
When all else fades,
My amazing dark night sky.

I find you there,
My Sophia dear,

Bethany Davis

My amazing dark night sky.

~July 26, 2015

The Place I Long

The day draws near, my heart, my love,
When in your arms I'll be once more,
And all the waiting and all the pain,
Is worth this soon return.

And if I come to where you are,
Or if you come to me,
There is one place I want to be,
And it's both here and there.

The place I long and wish to be,
The place to which I return,
That place is not far away,
Nor is it ever near.

For where I long and wish to be,
The centre of my world,
Is in your strong and loving arms,
That's where I soon will be.

~July 30, 2015

Bethany Davis

Plastic Roses

When even plastic roses fade to grey,
And memories are all long gone,
And life blooms forth from forgotten graves,
The living all long gone,
When bones have turned to hidden dust,
The muscles all long gone,
And all my thoughts have gone to grey,
Their colours all long gone,
Still will my love still be true to you,
When we are both long gone,
For in you I've found my heart, my soul,
And will love you evermore.

~August 1, 2015

Bethany Davis

Depths of You

My love grows stronger,
As each day passes,
And I come to know you more,
The depths of you,
The depths of me,
The depths no one else can see,
And as I hunger,
And as I long,
For you more every day,
I know your love,
And know you true,
And know you long for me.

There is no other,
In all of time,
That I have ever sought,
What we have,
Beyond all words,
No other can ever know,
In your arms,
Is like no place,
I know or can ever know,
And your lips on mine,
And mine on yours,
There's nothing sweeter known.

You my love,
Bring me joy,
And know my inner thoughts,
And only you,
I trust that much,
Whom knows my inner soul,
Safe and secure,
When with my love,
Who holds me close to her,
On the street,
Or in our bed,
With you I want to be.

Bethany Davis

Your voice my love,
It is a caress,
That runs all along my skin,
And your hands,
Upon my skin,
Are like nothing else on earth,
Your lips my dear,
Upon my breasts,
Are so beyond my words,
And only you,
Can bring me joy,
With just one little look.

My love grows stronger,
As each day passes,
And I come to know you more,
The depths of you,
The depths of me,
The depths no one else can see,
And as I hunger,
And as I long,
For you more every day,
I know your love,
And know you true,
And know you long for me.

~August 9, 2015

Mist and Smoke

Through the months since we last kissed,
All the distance and the time,
How we wished and how we pined,
The longing for one touch,
And chasms wide with mist and smoke,
And all that stood between,
To lie once more in your loving arms,
To know your loving kiss,
Here you are, my heart, my soul,
My dark dark night sky,
You came to me and lit my world,
My moon and stars and love,
Distance might make the heart grow strong,
And time makes all things change,
But in your arms the distance fades,
And time does not remain,
A bridge you crossed the chasm wide,
And traveled here to me,
No small thing, my heart, my soul,
My brave and amazing love,
Sophia you are my heart's delight,
And all the time is past,
For in your arms once more I lie,
Your kiss I know once more,
And chasms wide with mist and smoke,
And all that stood between,
Is in the past and done and gone,
And together we are once more.

~August 13, 2015

Bethany Davis

ABOUT THE AUTHOR

Bethany Davis currently resides in Colorado and waits and dreams of the day when her true love in Saskatchewan is with her every day. Previously she lived in Wyoming. She currently works in an operations role for a technology company. She is the proud mother of a fey creature in the form of a cat, adopted mother of a bird in the form of a cat, is a part time vegan and part time meat connoisseur, and a walker of edges. Her life pursuit is to find beauty in all things. Bethany has been writing poetry and prose most of her life, among other pursuits.

www.ingramcontent.com/pod-product-compliance
Lightning Source LLC
Chambersburg PA
CBHW020623300426
44113CB00007B/755